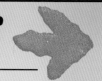

GRAPHIC DINOSAURS

ALLOSAURUS

THE STRANGE LIZARD

ILLUSTRATED BY TERRY RILEY

PowerKiDS
press.
New York

Published in 2010 by The Rosen Publishing Group, Inc.
29 East 21st Street, New York, NY 10010

Designed and produced by
David West Books

Designed and written by Rob Shone
Editor: Ronne Randall
U.S. Editor: Kara Murray
Consultant: Steve Parker, Senior Scientific Fellow, Zoological Society of London
Photographic credits: 5t, Mess of Pottage; 5m, Tomomarusan; 30, Micha L. Rieser.

Library of Congress Cataloging-in-Publication Data

Shone, Rob.
Allosaurus : the strange lizard / Rob Shone ; illustrated by Terry Riley.
p. cm. — (Graphic dinosaurs)
Includes index.
ISBN 978-1-4358-8588-2 (lib. bdg.) — ISBN 978-1-4358-8592-9 (pbk.) —
ISBN 978-1-4358-8593-6 (6-pack)
1. Allosaurus—Juvenile literature. I. Riley, Terry, ill. II. Title.
QE862.S3S4446 2009
567.912—dc22
                                                      2009016045

Manufactured in China

CONTENTS

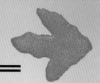

WHAT IS AN ALLOSAURUS?

ALLOSAURUS MEANS "STRANGE LIZARD"

◄ Allosaurus's teeth had wavy edges, like steak knives. This made it easier to cut through meat. They fell out easily but were replaced throughout the Allosaurus's life.

◄ The horns over Allosaurus's eyes would have helped protect its eyes in combat. They would also have acted as a sun shield.

◄ Allosaurus's tail was held straight and stiff. It acted as a balance when Allosaurus walked or ran.

◄ Allosaurus's eyes did not point forward, so it would have found it hard to judge distances.

◄ Allosaurus had a good sense of smell.

◄ Allosaurus's arms were short but powerful. The three fingers of each hand ended in a large, curved claw.

◄ Allosaurus had a very strong skull, but its bite was not very strong for the size of its jaws and teeth.

◄ Allosaurus had a row of riblike bones called gastralia protecting its stomach.

ALLOSAURUS WAS A DINOSAUR THAT LIVED AROUND 155 MILLION TO 145 MILLION YEARS AGO, DURING THE JURASSIC PERIOD. FOSSILS OF ITS SKELETON HAVE BEEN FOUND IN NORTH AMERICA, AFRICA, AND EUROPE.

An adult Allosaurus measured up to 38 feet (12 m) long and 16.5 feet (5 m) high and weighed 4.5 tons (4,082 kg).

JURASSIC LANDSCAPE

Allosaurus was the most successful large meat-eating dinosaur of the late Jurassic period. It lived in flat river valleys and forests filled with pine trees, cycads, and tree ferns. Allosaurus would have hunted the large plant eaters that lived with it, like Stegosaurus, Camptosaurus, and Dryosaurus.

A museum display showing an Allosaurus attacking a Stegosaurus.

SAUROPOD HUNTERS

Many different types of sauropods (four-legged plant-eating dinosaurs with long necks and tails) lived alongside Allosauruses. Adult sauropods were too big to be attacked by Allosauruses. They could have hunted sauropods that were young or sick and weak. Allosauruses might even have hunted in packs, as wolves and lions do today.

A lion watches as a herd of wildebeest runs past. Allosauruses have been called the Lions of the Jurassic.

On an Allosaurus, this claw bone would have been covered with the same material found on a horn.

PART ONE... DAY ONE

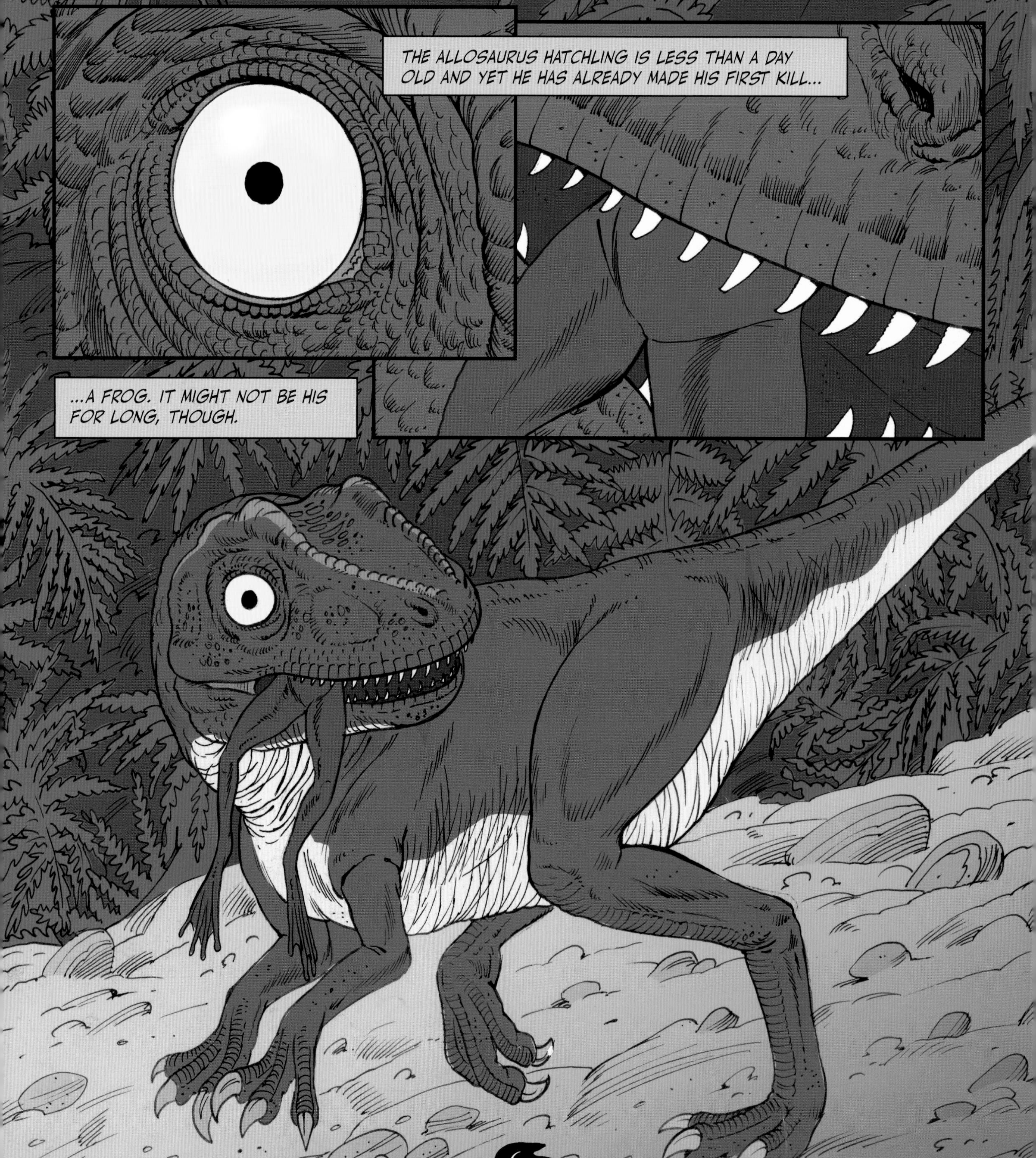

HIS BROTHERS AND SISTERS WANT TO SHARE IT.

THEY HAVE HIM SURROUNDED...

...BUT HE WILL NOT GIVE UP THE FROG WITHOUT A FIGHT.

GNAHH!!

A SUDDEN NOISE PUTS AN END TO THE FIGHTING. IT MAY BE THEIR MOTHER, BACK WITH FOOD.

IT IS NOT THEIR MOTHER. A HERD OF CAMPTOSAURUSES CHARGES STRAIGHT AT THE HATCHLINGS.

ROUHHAHH!!

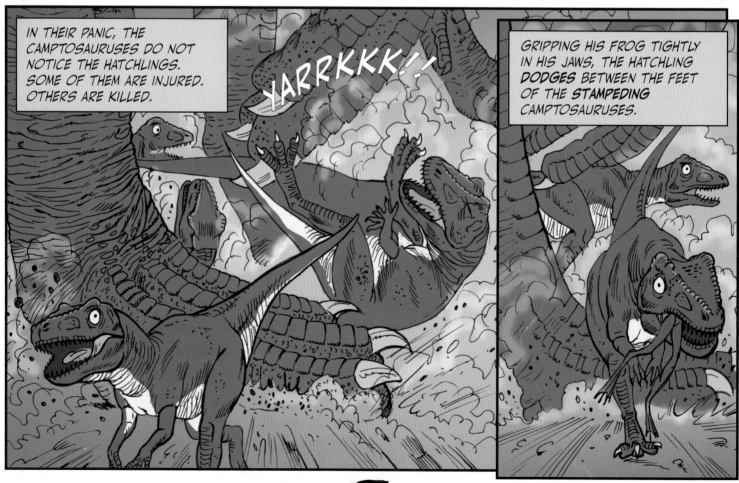

IN THEIR PANIC, THE CAMPTOSAURUSES DO NOT NOTICE THE HATCHLINGS. SOME OF THEM ARE INJURED. OTHERS ARE KILLED.

YARRKKK!!

GRIPPING HIS FROG TIGHTLY IN HIS JAWS, THE HATCHLING **DODGES** BETWEEN THE FEET OF THE **STAMPEDING** CAMPTOSAURUSES.

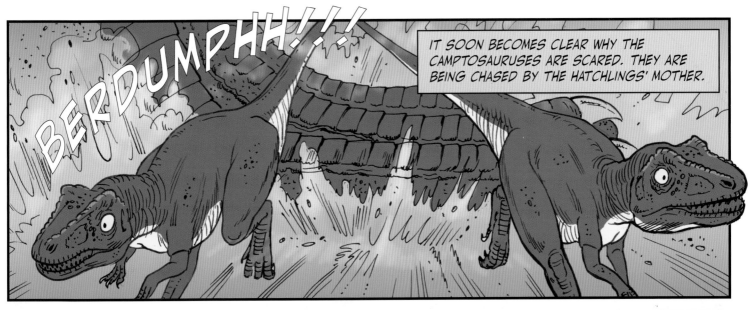

BERDUMPHH!!!!

IT SOON BECOMES CLEAR WHY THE CAMPTOSAURUSES ARE SCARED. THEY ARE BEING CHASED BY THE HATCHLINGS' MOTHER.

SHE LUNGES AT ONE OF THE CAMPTOSAURUSES AND BRINGS IT DOWN.

THE OTHER CAMPTOSAURUSES DO NOT STOP RUNNING. THE HATCHLING SEES A HOLE IN THE GROUND...

...AND DIVES INTO IT.

OUTSIDE, THE CAMPTOSAURUSES RUSH PAST. THE HATCHLING FEELS SAFE IN THE COOL, DARK HOLE. HE STARES INTO THE BLACKNESS...

...AND HALF A DOZEN SETS OF SMALL, SHINY EYES STARE BACK.

THE HOLE IS THE BURROW OF A LARGE FAMILY OF FRUITAFOSSORS. THESE TINY MAMMALS ARE NOT HAPPY TO SEE AN INTRUDER IN THEIR HOME.

THERE ARE TOO MANY FRUITAFOSSORS FOR THE HATCHLING.

ARRRKK!

WITH SNAPPING JAWS, THE ANGRY INSECT EATERS CHASE THE HATCHLING OUT OF THEIR BURROW. HE DASHES FROM THE HOLE, LEAVING HIS FROG BEHIND.

HE DOES NOT STOP RUNNING UNTIL HE JOINS HIS BROTHERS AND SISTERS.

THE HATCHLINGS ARE WATCHING WHILE THEIR MOTHER FEEDS ON THE DEAD CAMPTOSAURUS. THEY CANNOT GET TOO CLOSE OR THEIR MOTHER MIGHT KILL THEM, TOO. THEY MUST WAIT FOR THEIR TURN TO EAT.

BEFORE LONG, THE ALLOSAURUS FINISHES HER MEAL AND LETS THE HATCHLINGS HAVE THEIRS. THE YOUNG ALLOSAURUS REMEMBERS HIS LOST FROG AND EATS GREEDILY. HE WILL MAKE MANY MORE KILLS IN THE YEARS TO COME.

PART TWO... THE HOT SPRINGS

THE ALLOSAURUS IS NOW THREE YEARS OLD AND IS 10 FEET (3 M) LONG. HE IS HUNTING A HERD OF SMALL PLANT-EATING OTHNIELIAS. THEY HAVE LED HIM INTO A STEAM-FILLED VALLEY OF HOT SPRINGS, AND GEYSERS THAT SEND JETS OF BOILING WATER INTO THE AIR. THE YOUNG ALLOSAURUS CREEPS CLOSER TO THE OTHNIELIAS BUT HAS TO BE CAREFUL. THEY HAVE A BODYGUARD.

WHOOSH!!!

THE OTHNIELIAS ARE FEEDING CLOSE TO A HESPEROSAURUS. THE SPIKES AT THE END OF ITS TAIL CAN BE DEADLY.

THE ALLOSAURUS LEAVES HIS HIDING PLACE AND MOVES SLOWLY TOWARD THE OTHNIELIAS.

AT THAT MOMENT A CERATOSAURUS BURSTS FROM THE TREES. LIKE THE ALLOSAURUS, HE IS HUNTING, BUT NOT THE OTHNIELIAS. HE IS HUNTING THE HESPEROSAURUS.

WROARR!!

THE OTHNIELIAS RUN IN PANIC. ONE OF THEM RUSHES PAST THE ALLOSAURUS.

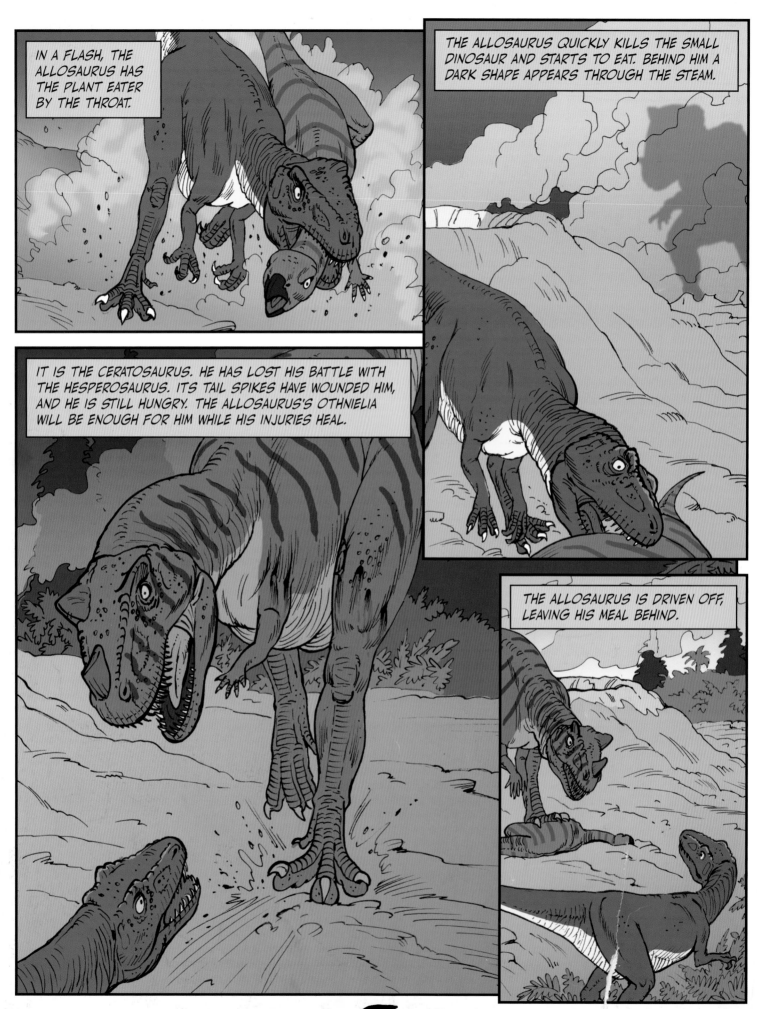

IN A FLASH, THE ALLOSAURUS HAS THE PLANT EATER BY THE THROAT.

THE ALLOSAURUS QUICKLY KILLS THE SMALL DINOSAUR AND STARTS TO EAT. BEHIND HIM A DARK SHAPE APPEARS THROUGH THE STEAM.

IT IS THE CERATOSAURUS. HE HAS LOST HIS BATTLE WITH THE HESPEROSAURUS. ITS TAIL SPIKES HAVE WOUNDED HIM, AND HE IS STILL HUNGRY. THE ALLOSAURUS'S OTHNIELIA WILL BE ENOUGH FOR HIM WHILE HIS INJURIES HEAL.

THE ALLOSAURUS IS DRIVEN OFF, LEAVING HIS MEAL BEHIND.

THE WOUNDED DINOSAUR BEGINS TO FEED ON THE STOLEN PREY.

THE CERATOSAURUS STOPS EATING. HE WATCHES AS STEAM AND HOT WATER BUBBLE UP FROM THE ROCKS BESIDE HIM.

BERLBOOP!

THE MEAT EATER IS STANDING NEXT TO A GEYSER. IT SUDDENLY **ERUPTS**, SHOOTING BOILING WATER AND **SCALDING** STEAM HIGH INTO THE AIR.

BARROOSHHH!!!

THE YOUNG ALLOSAURUS HAS BEEN LUCKY. HE COULD HAVE BEEN CAUGHT BY THE ERUPTING GEYSER INSTEAD OF THE CERATOSAURUS. HE IS STILL HUNGRY, THOUGH. HE TURNS TO SEARCH FOR THE REST OF THE OTHNIELIAS. THIS TIME THE HESPEROSAURUS MIGHT NOT BE THERE TO PROTECT THEM.

THE ALLOSAURUS IS NOW 12 YEARS OLD AND IS 20 FEET (6 M) LONG. IT IS THE DRY SEASON. FOOD AND WATER ARE SCARCE FOR BOTH PLANT EATERS AND MEAT EATERS. THE ALLOSAURUS HAS NOT EATEN FOR SEVERAL DAYS AND IS VERY HUNGRY.

A PAIR OF COELURUSES, SEARCHING FOR LIZARDS TO EAT, RUN WHEN THEY SEE THE ALLOSAURUS COMING. HE IS NOT INTERESTED IN THEM. HE SNIFFS THE AIR...

...AND SMELLS FOOD.

NOT FAR AWAY, A HERD OF APATOSAURUSES IS TRAVELING ALONG A DRY RIVERBED IN SEARCH OF WATER. THE YOUNG ALLOSAURUS WATCHES THEM. KILLING SUCH LARGE PREY WILL NOT BE EASY, BUT HE DESPERATELY NEEDS TO EAT.

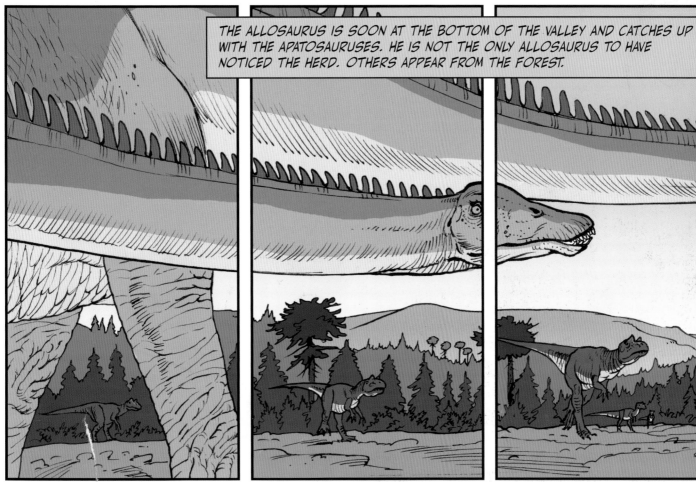

THE ALLOSAURUS IS SOON AT THE BOTTOM OF THE VALLEY AND CATCHES UP WITH THE APATOSAURUSES. HE IS NOT THE ONLY ALLOSAURUS TO HAVE NOTICED THE HERD. OTHERS APPEAR FROM THE FOREST.

APATOSAURUSES ARE TOO HEAVY TO RUN QUICKLY. A STEADY TROT IS ENOUGH FOR THE ALLOSAURUS TO KEEP UP WITH THEM.

HE IS LOOKING FOR A WAY INTO THE MIDDLE OF THE HERD. THAT IS WHERE THE YOUNG APATOSAURUSES ARE. THEY ARE WEAKER AND WILL BE EASIER TO KILL, BUT THEY ARE PROTECTED BY THE ADULTS. A BLOW FROM THEIR LONG, THIN TAIL CAN BREAK BONES, WHILE THEIR POWERFUL NECK CAN SEND AN ALLOSAURUS CRASHING TO THE GROUND.

SEVERAL ALLOSAURUSES HAVE JOINED THE CHASE. THEY ARE NOT USED TO HUNTING TOGETHER AND SNAP AT EACH OTHER.

RARRSH!!

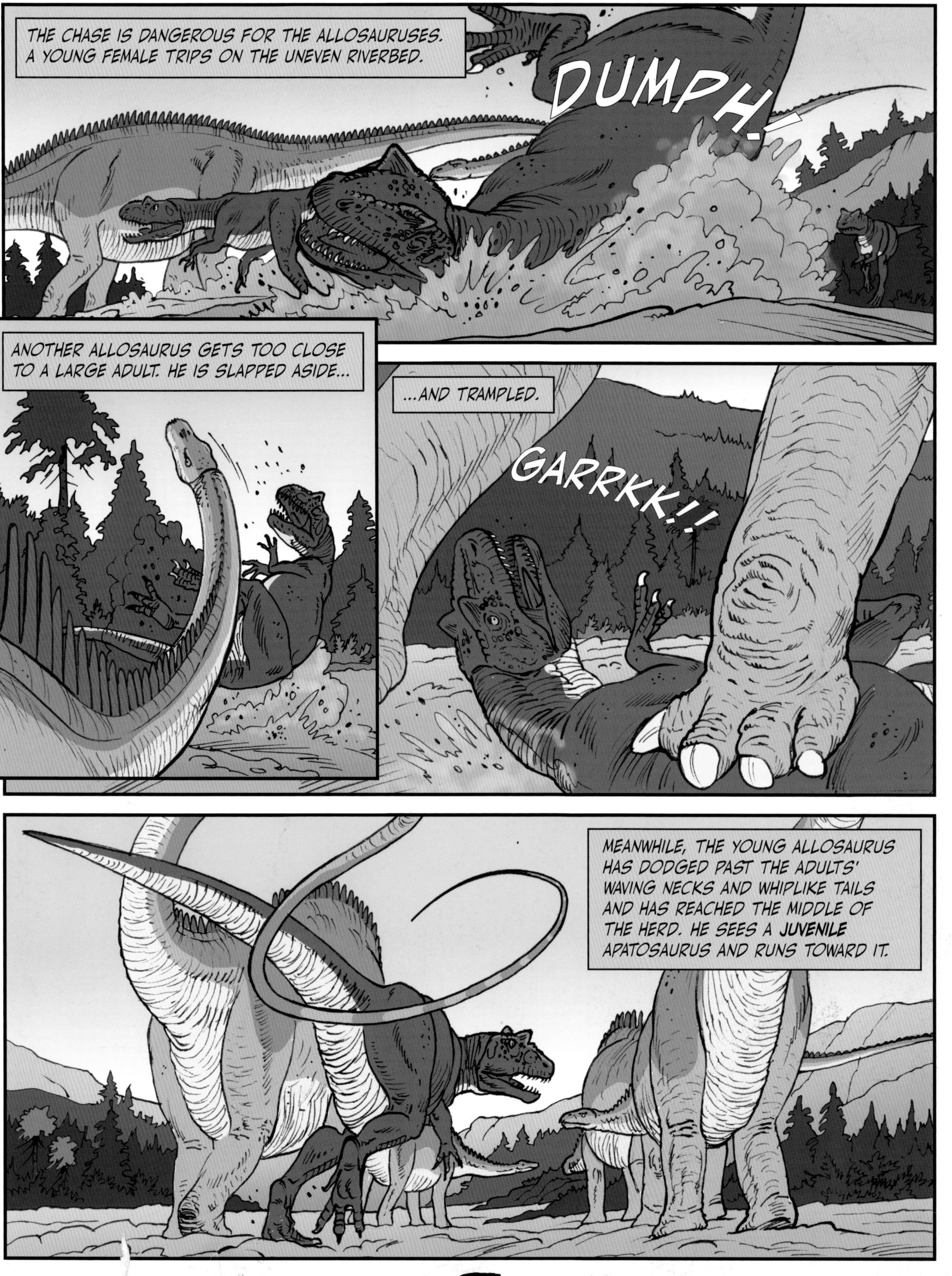
THE CHASE IS DANGEROUS FOR THE ALLOSAURUSES. A YOUNG FEMALE TRIPS ON THE UNEVEN RIVERBED.
DUMPH!
ANOTHER ALLOSAURUS GETS TOO CLOSE TO A LARGE ADULT. HE IS SLAPPED ASIDE...
...AND TRAMPLED.
GARRKK!!!
MEANWHILE, THE YOUNG ALLOSAURUS HAS DODGED PAST THE ADULTS' WAVING NECKS AND WHIPLIKE TAILS AND HAS REACHED THE MIDDLE OF THE HERD. HE SEES A **JUVENILE** APATOSAURUS AND RUNS TOWARD IT.

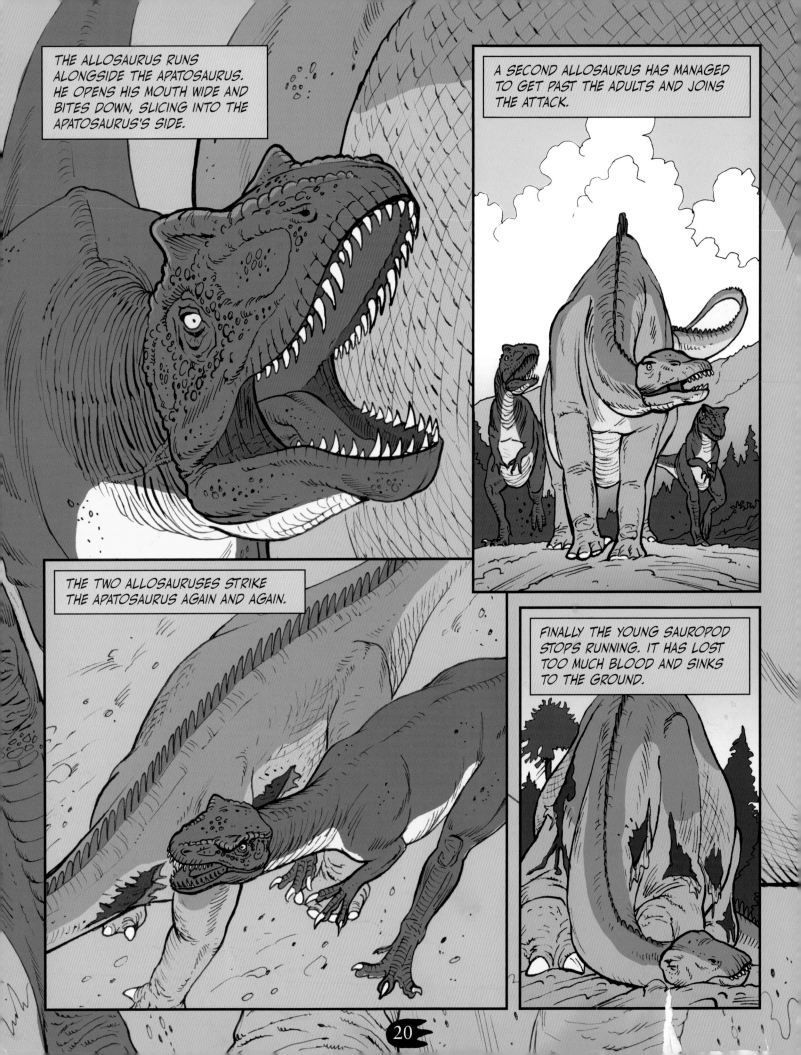

THE ALLOSAURUS RUNS ALONGSIDE THE APATOSAURUS. HE OPENS HIS MOUTH WIDE AND BITES DOWN, SLICING INTO THE APATOSAURUS'S SIDE.

A SECOND ALLOSAURUS HAS MANAGED TO GET PAST THE ADULTS AND JOINS THE ATTACK.

THE TWO ALLOSAURUSES STRIKE THE APATOSAURUS AGAIN AND AGAIN.

FINALLY THE YOUNG SAUROPOD STOPS RUNNING. IT HAS LOST TOO MUCH BLOOD AND SINKS TO THE GROUND.

THE YOUNG ALLOSAURUSES
CLOSE IN TO KILL THEIR PREY.

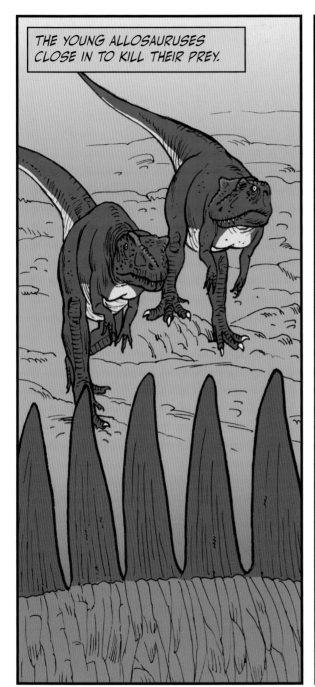

THEY CANNOT EAT JUST YET. THE LARGEST ALLOSAURUS HAS
CLAIMED THE DEAD APATOSAURUS FOR HERSELF. THE OTHERS
MUST WAIT THEIR TURN. LUCKILY, THERE IS ENOUGH MEAT ON
THE APATOSAURUS TO FEED THEM ALL.

THE ALLOSAURUS
THAT TRIPPED LIMPS AWAY PAINFULLY.
SHE WILL NOT STAY TO TAKE HER SHARE OF THE
SAUROPOD. IF THE OTHERS SEE THAT SHE IS
HURT, THEY MIGHT ATTACK AND KILL HER. NEARBY,
LYING ON THE GROUND, IS THE ALLOSAURUS
THAT WAS TRAMPLED. HE WILL NEVER HUNT AGAIN.

PART FOUR

ON GUARD

THE ALLOSAURUS HAS EATEN PART OF A CAMPTOSAURUS HE HAS CAUGHT AND IS ASLEEP. AT 25, HE IS NOW OLD FOR AN ALLOSAURUS...

...BUT HE IS STILL STRONG AND DANGEROUS. A FLOCK OF KEPODACTYLUSES CIRCLES ABOVE HIM. THEY SEE THE CAMPTOSAURUS ON THE RIVERBANK AND WANT A PIECE OF IT.

THE KEPODACTYLUSES SWOOP OUT OF THE SKY AND DOWN ONTO THE BODY OF THE DEAD DINOSAUR.

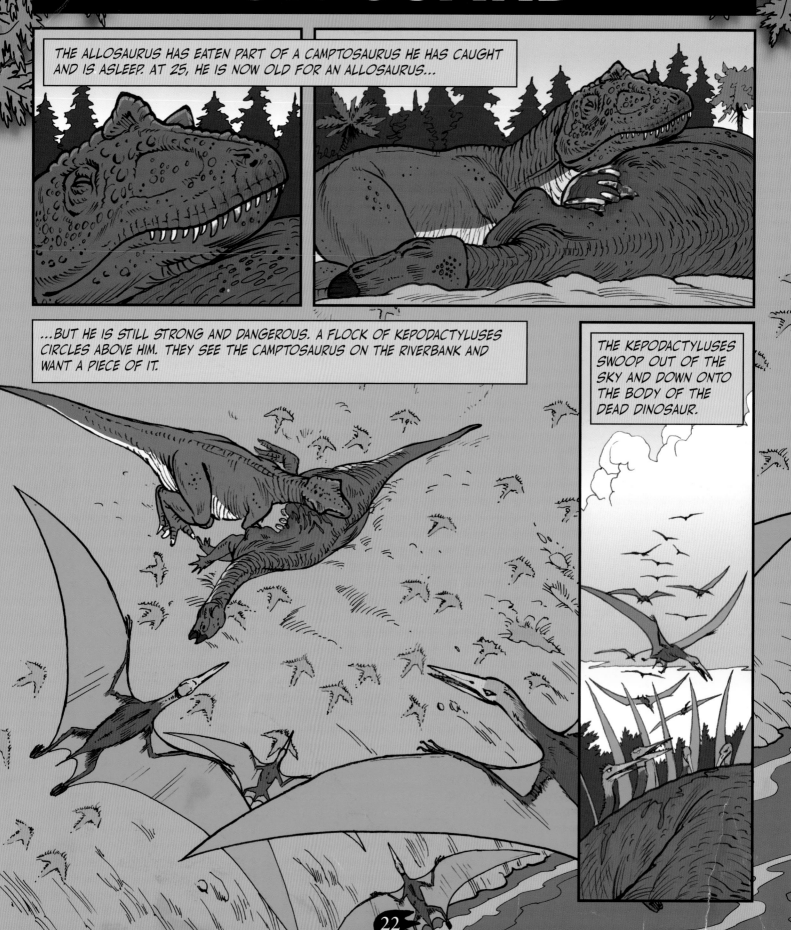

A PAIR OF ORNITHOLESTES FOLLOW THE KEPODACTYLUSES. THEY KNOW THAT THE FLYING REPTILES CAN OFTEN LEAD THEM TO FOOD.

THE MEAT-EATING ORNITHOLESTES RUSH AT THE KEPODACTYLUSES, SENDING THEM FLAPPING INTO THE AIR. THEIR CRIES DO NOT WAKE THE ALLOSAURUS. HIS EARS CAN ONLY DETECT LOW-PITCHED SOUNDS.

ARRKK!!

ARRKK!!

THE ORNITHOLESTES ENJOY A FREE MEAL WHILE THE ALLOSAURUS SLEEPS.

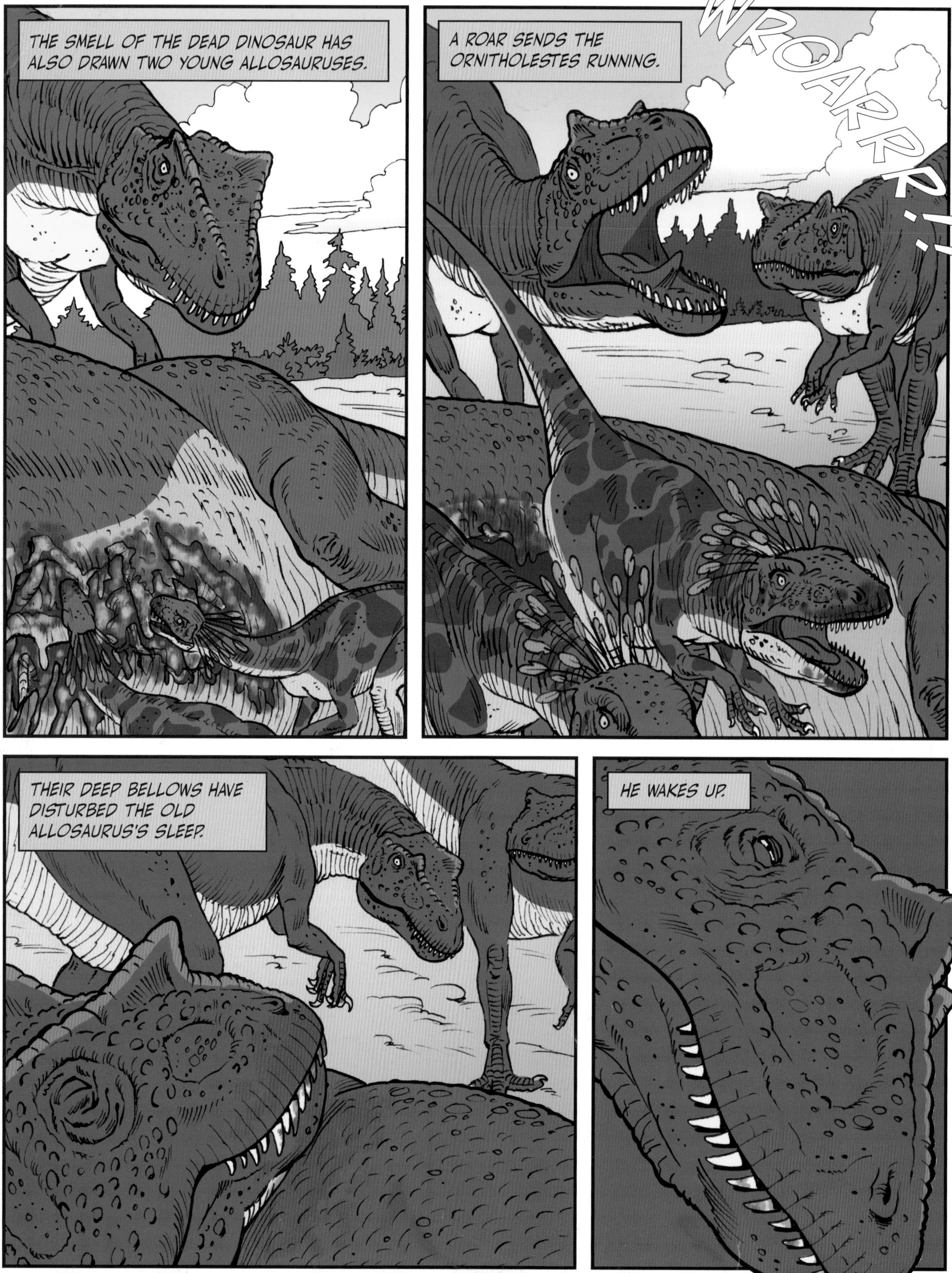
THE SMELL OF THE DEAD DINOSAUR HAS ALSO DRAWN TWO YOUNG ALLOSAURUSES.
A ROAR SENDS THE ORNITHOLESTES RUNNING.
WROARRR!!!
THEIR DEEP BELLOWS HAVE DISTURBED THE OLD ALLOSAURUS'S SLEEP.
HE WAKES UP.

THE ALLOSAURUSES HISS AND ROAR AT EACH OTHER. THE OLD ALLOSAURUS CAN HANDLE ONE YOUNG ALLOSAURUS. TWO OF THEM TOGETHER, THOUGH, ARE TOO DANGEROUS TO FIGHT. IT LOOKS AS IF THE OLD ALLOSAURUS MUST GIVE UP HIS KILL.

GRAHHH!!

SUDDENLY, THE TWO YOUNG ALLOSAURUSES LET OUT A CRY AND RUN.

THE OLD ALLOSAURUS TURNS TO SEE WHAT HAS SCARED THEM.

A HERD OF CAMARASAURUSES ARE WALKING ALONG THE RIVER. THE OLD ALLOSAURUS AND HIS MEAL ARE IN THEIR WAY.

THE ALLOSAURUS STANDS GUARD OVER THE DEAD CAMPTOSAURUS AS THE CAMARASAURUSES PASS BY. HE HISSES AND ROARS AT THEM, WARNING THEM TO KEEP AWAY.

THE CAMARASAURUSES ALSO SEE THE ALLOSAURUS AS A THREAT. A LARGE ADULT BRUSHES THE ALLOSAURUS ASIDE WITH A BLOW FROM ITS POWERFUL NECK.

KRAAKK!!

WHILE THE STUNNED ALLOSAURUS STRUGGLES TO HIS FEET, THE HERD MOVES ON.

THE CAMARASAURUSES HAVE TRAMPLED THE BODY OF THE CAMPTOSAURUS INTO THE MUD.

THE ALLOSAURUS ROARS AFTER THE CAMARASAURUSES. HE IS SO ANGRY THAT HE DOES NOT NOTICE WHAT IS HAPPENING AT HIS FEET.

THE TIDE HAS TURNED AND THE RIVER IS RISING. HE WILL LOSE THE CAMPTOSAURUS IF HE DOES NOT ACT QUICKLY.

HE GRABS THE DINOSAUR WITH HIS JAWS AND TRIES TO DRAG IT OUT OF THE RIVER, BUT IT IS STUCK FAST IN THE MUD.

THE RIVER CURRENT IS TOO STRONG FOR THE ALLOSAURUS. HE SPLASHES THROUGH THE WATER TO DRY LAND, LEAVING THE CAMPTOSAURUS BEHIND.

BDOOSH!

HE WATCHES FROM THE BANK AS HIS MEAL SLOWLY DISAPPEARS BENEATH THE SURFACE OF THE WATER.

THE CAMPTOSAURUS HAS BECOME FOOD FOR THE FISH.

THE OLD ALLOSAURUS PLODS AWAY FROM THE RIVER. HE IS NOT TOO SAD TO LOSE THE CAMPTOSAURUS. HE HAD EATEN SOME OF IT. HE MAY EVEN COME BACK LATER WHEN THE TIDE HAS GONE OUT. THE FISH MIGHT NOT HAVE EATEN IT ALL. IN THE MEANTIME, HE GOES IN SEARCH OF SOMETHING TO KILL.

FOSSIL EVIDENCE

SCIENTISTS LEARN WHAT DINOSAURS MAY HAVE LOOKED LIKE BY STUDYING THEIR FOSSIL REMAINS. FOSSILS ARE FORMED WHEN THE HARD PARTS OF AN ANIMAL OR PLANT ARE BURIED AND TURN TO ROCK OVER THOUSANDS OF YEARS.

In 1991, a nearly complete fossilized skeleton of a male Allosaurus was found near Shell, Wyoming. The scientists who studied the fossil named the Allosaurus Big Al. They discovered that Big Al's life had been short and hard. He had broken bones in his tail and ribs and had diseases in his hips and claws. Big Al's broken bones had healed, but an **infected** toe had not. This would have stopped him from running and hunting. Big Al probably starved to death.

In 1996, another Allosaurus skeleton (left) was found in Wyoming. Scientists called this one Big Al Two. He was fully grown and had most of his bones. Like Big Al, some of them had been broken and had healed. Scientists had believed that such injuries might have killed a large dinosaur. But the healed bones proved that both Allosauruses had survived. These meat eaters were tougher than anyone thought.

ANIMAL GALLERY

ALL THESE ANIMALS APPEAR IN THE STORY.

Othnielia
"Othniel's dinosaur"
Length: 5 ft (1.5 m)
A small, fast-moving
plant eater.

Ornitholestes
"Bird robber"
Length: 6.5 ft (2 m)
A meat-eating
dinosaur.

Kepodactylus
"Garden finger"
Wingspan: 8 ft (2.5 m)
A flying reptile.

Coelurus
"Hollow tail"
Length: 8 ft (2.5 m)
A small meat-eating
dinosaur that gets its
name from the hollow
bones in its tail.

Hesperosaurus
"Western lizard"
Length: 20 ft (6 m)
A plant-eating dinosaur and
smaller relative of the similar
Stegosaurus.

Camptosaurus
"Bent lizard"
Length: 26 ft (8 m)
A medium-sized plant eater.
It gets its name from the shape
its back made when it stood on
all four feet.

Ceratosaurus
"Horned lizard"
Length: 17.5 ft (5 m)
Ceratosaurus was a medium-
sized meat-eating dinosaur.
Its tail was more flexible than
those of most other meat-eaters.

Apatosaurus
"Deceptive lizard"
Length: 75 ft (23 m)
A large plant eater. When it was found, some of
its bones were thought to belong to a type of
marine reptile, which is how it got its name.

Camarasaurus
"Chambered lizard"
Length: 60 ft (18 m)
A plant-eating sauropod. Camarasaurus gets its
name from the holes in its backbone and skull,
which made them light but strong.

GLOSSARY

 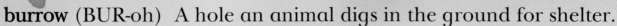

burrow (BUR-oh) A hole an animal digs in the ground for shelter.

dodges (DOJ-ez) Avoids an object by moving quickly.

erupts (ih-RUPTS) Breaks out suddenly.

fossils (FO-sulz) The remains of living things that have turned to rock.

infected (in-FEK-ted) Diseased.

Jurassic period (ju-RA-sik PIR-ee-ud) The time between 200 million years ago and 145 million years ago.

juvenile (JOO-veh-ny-uhl) A young animal that is not fully grown.

scalding (SKAWL-ding) Very hot, as of water or steam.

stampeding (stam-PEED-ing) Running in a wild panic.

INDEX

Web Sites
Due to the changing nature of Internet links, the Rosen Publishing Group, Inc., has developed an online list of Web sites related to the subject of this book. This site is updated regularly. Please use this link to access the list:
www.powerkidslinks.com/gdino/allo/